HR INFORMATION SYSTEMS:
STAND AND DELIVER

Other titles from IES:

From Admin to Strategy: the changing face of the HR Function
Tamkin P, Barber L, Dench S
IES Report 332, 1997. ISBN 1-85184-263-2

Changing Roles for Senior Managers
Kettley P, Strebler M T
IES Report 327, 1997. ISBN 1-85184-255-1

Outsourcing: a Flexible Option for the Future?
Reilly P, Tamkin P
IES Report 320, 1997. ISBN 1-85184-247-0

Human Resource Planning: an Introduction
Reilly P
IES Report 312, 1996. ISBN 1-85184-238-1

Measuring and Monitoring Absence from Work
Seccombe I
IES Report 288, 1995. ISBN 1-85184-214-4

Measuring the Personnel Function
Hirsh W, Bevan S, Barber L
IES Report 286, 1995. ISBN 1-85184-212-8

A catalogue of these and over 100 other titles is available from IES.

the | **INSTITUTE**
for | **EMPLOYMENT**
| **STUDIES**

HR INFORMATION SYSTEMS:
STAND AND DELIVER

Dilys Robinson

A study supported by the
IES Co-operative Research Programme

Report 335

Published by:

THE INSTITUTE FOR EMPLOYMENT STUDIES
Mantell Building
University of Sussex
Brighton BN1 9RF
UK

Tel.   + 44 (0) 1273 686751
Fax   + 44 (0) 1273 690430

British Cataloguing-in-Publication Data

A catalogue record for this publication is available from the British Library

ISBN 1-85184-261-6

Printed in Great Britain by Microgen UK Ltd

The Institute for Employment Studies

IES is an independent, international and apolitical centre of research and consultancy in human resource issues. It works closely with employers in the manufacturing, service and public sectors, government departments, agencies, professional and employee bodies, and foundations. Since it was established over 25 years ago the Institute has been a focus of knowledge and practical experience in employment and training policy, the operation of labour markets and human resource planning and development. IES is a not-for-profit organisation which has a multidisciplinary staff of over 50. IES expertise is available to all organisations through research, consultancy and publications.

IES aims to help bring about sustainable improvements in employment policy and human resource management. IES achieves this by increasing the understanding and improving the practice of key decision makers in policy bodies and employing organisations.

The IES Co-operative Research Programme

This report is the product of a study supported by the IES Co-operative Research Programme, through which a group of IES Subscribers finance, and often participate in, applied research on employment issues. The members of the CRP are:

BAA plc
Barclays Bank plc
British Broadcasting Corporation
British Steel plc
BT plc
Cabinet Office (OPS)
Department of Transport
Electricity Association
Glaxo Wellcome plc
Guardian Insurance
Halifax plc

HM Customs & Excise
Inland Revenue
Lloyds TSB Group
Marks & Spencer plc
National Westminster Bank plc
Post Office
Rolls-Royce plc
J Sainsbury plc
Shell UK Ltd
Unilever UK (Holdings) Ltd
Woolwich Building Society

Acknowledgements

This study has been a pleasurable one to conduct. We are indebted to the patient co-operation of the six organisations who allowed themselves to be scrutinised and questioned, at length, about their use of computerised Human Resources information systems. Thanks are also due to the system suppliers' representatives (from IBM, SAP (UK), Peterborough Software and PeopleSoft), who offered some perceptive comments.

Several people at IES have contributed to this study. Emma Pollard reviewed the recent literature, Gwen Leeming made the report presentable, Peter Herriot helped to shape the report and Andy Davidson turned it into a publication.

Finally, thanks are due to the members of the Co-operative Research Programme for providing the funding and support for this study.

Contents

Introduction

Most medium or large organisations have a computerised Human Resources (HR) information system, and for many HR practitioners the use of such systems has become a matter of daily routine. Many large organisations, after using a mainframe system for perhaps ten or twelve years, are considering abandoning it in favour of one of the new, state-of-the-art (and expensive) models. For several years, HR information systems have been attractively packaged and slickly presented — yet, back at the workplace, they often fail to live up to their promises. Implementation delays, difficulties with gathering data, technical hitches and inadequate reporting facilities lead to disillusionment, frustration and a feeling that expectations have not been met.

Table 1: Is there a difference?

Personnel records systems	HR management systems
● Owned by the HR department	● Managed by the HR department, but owned by the organisation
● Maintained by HR	● Maintained by HR and line management
● Limited or no access outside HR	● Access by line management and (possibly) individuals
● Fed by paper or via a limited network	● Fed via intranet, e-mail and workflow
● Limited assistance to HR processes	● Integral to HR processes
● Limited by boundaries of location and geography	● Boundaries no object

Source: IES 1997

HR practitioners are also accused of failing to use information technology (IT) properly — indeed, of being IT illiterate in comparison with other functions. HR information systems are perceived as personnel records systems, rather than management tools to inform decision-making (see table 1). In turn, HR practitioners have argued that they are often last in the queue when IT resources are distributed, that projects to implement HR information systems are IT-led, and that the systems themselves are inflexible and failing to deliver.

In an attempt to disentangle myth from reality, this study has enlisted the help of six large organisations, all of whom have had an HR information system for years, and some of whom are looking for, or implementing, a newer model. The wider picture, as presented by the results of several surveys, is also examined, as is the supplier's perspective. Finally, some practical advice is offered, drawn from the good practice that has been encountered while conducting this study.

This report has the following structure:

- Chapter one identifies the themes that occur most frequently in discussions about HR information systems.
- Chapter two presents the case studies.
- Chapter three looks at the wider picture.
- Chapter four gives the supplier's perspective.
- Chapter five re-visits the themes and discusses whether they are supported by the evidence gathered by this study.
- Chapter six offers some practical advice, based on the findings of this study, to organisations which are considering buying and implementing a new system.
- Finally, there is a glossary, and a references and further reading section.

1 IT and HR — What People Say

This chapter examines some of the common themes that occur frequently, both in discussions with HR practitioners, IT experts and line managers, and in the available literature on the subject. Inevitably, some of the themes are linked, and some overlap, but they nevertheless form a useful basis for discussion.

HR: the poor relation

One claim frequently voiced by HR practitioners is that IT resources are dished out to everyone else in the organisation before HR gets a share. In particular, any area with a direct customer interface gets priority — partly to impress, but mainly to enable the organisation to respond directly and efficiently to requests for information and customer orders. Even behind the scenes, however, HR complains of being a Cinderella service in IT terms. Finance departments are especially likely to be suspected of grabbing an unfairly large share of the IT budget.

HR information system, but IT led

Expertise in evaluating and implementing computerised systems traditionally sat in IT departments. HR practitioners sometimes claim, as a result, that their systems were chosen on grounds that had little to do with functionality and ease of use. Instead, technical considerations (such as response times and hardware or operating system compatibility) dominated. In addition, a system produced by a supplier known to the organisation was often preferred over the system considered most acceptable by HR. The comparative technological naivety of HR practitioners made them vulnerable to persuasion by the IT function, and their inexperience at project management tended to mean that they had a back seat in planning and executing the implementation of the system. An OASIG study (1996), for example, which looked at a wide range of IT investments by organisations (not just HR information systems) found that most investments in IT are still technology-led.

To compound the problem, integrated payroll and personnel systems tended to be dominated by payroll, with implementation being geared towards the overarching priority of getting payroll to run accurately and on time.

Where is the business justification?

One criticism laid at the door of HR is that it fails, as a function, to justify its existence and value to the organisation — one symptom of this failure being the purchase of expensive HR information systems without any attempt to quantify the benefits they will bring. At best, there are vague promises of 'improved information' and an expectation, which usually fails to materialise, of staff savings. This apparent laxity adds to the perception that HR is buying the system for its own use, rather than for the benefit of the business. Even worse, once the system is up and running, HR seems to lack the will to 'sell' it to the rest of the organisation, despite earlier promises of a roll-out to managers. It remains in the HR department, regarded with some suspicion by outsiders as a system 'monster' that has to be fed with data, usually on paper forms.

HR information systems threaten jobs

HR information systems are often sold to organisations on the basis that they will remove much of the routine drudgery from HR practitioners, and leave them free to pursue higher and more strategic goals. They could, for example, become internal consultants, or enhance their roles by involvement in major HR initiatives. This does, however, imply that some jobs at a routine or junior level may no longer be needed. Similarly, payroll systems are sometimes perceived as putting the jobs of payroll clerks at risk. Any implementation which fails to recognise such fears could risk running into difficulties, as people with a negative stake in the system could actively try to undermine it.

Routine administration? Over to the line

This theme is heard frequently, and not only in the context of the maintenance of records on the HR information system. Line managers are increasingly expected to carry out many of the functions frequently performed by specialists, such as budget management, absence monitoring and recruiting. The argument is that line managers need information about their employees, and are in the best position to know when their personal or job details change — so they should also take responsibility for entering these details onto the HR information system. Unfortunately, the beleaguered line manager, faced with a system that does not produce the required reports, and which is difficult to use, is unlikely to perceive any benefit in this unequal exchange. The fact that line managers often perceive that service they receive from HR to be poor, or irrelevant, is another factor predisposing them towards a mistrust of HR information systems.

System expertise: the death knell to a career in HR

Technical skills, and in particular the ability to understand and manipulate the HR information system, are traditionally not rated highly in HR. In many organisations, becoming an expert user seems to pigeon-hole the HR practitioner, who then finds it difficult to get back into 'mainstream' HR. Ironically, although HR information system skills are not considered a core competency for HR, any individual with these skills is not given the opportunity to develop, as there is also a recognition that it is necessary to have at least one system expert in the department. The 'expert', rather than being respected as would happen in other departments, is then put in the frustrating position of being bypassed for career opportunities, because his or her skills are perceived as a necessary evil. This attitude appears to be particularly prevalent at senior levels, as this quotation from Kossek *et al.* (1994) illustrates:

> 'Hierarchical level has been found to be negatively related to the use and acceptance of information systems. The higher the position in HR, the more negative the attitudes toward the HR Information System since its use will be viewed as a clerical activity that will do little to enhance HR's reputation.'

Data input is also perceived as a low status job in the organisation, and tends to be delegated to clerks and secretaries, who are sometimes relatively new to the organisation. There are two inevitable results:

- low data quality
- the system being blamed for input errors.

But where is the vision?

One criticism frequently laid at the door of HR is that systems are purchased and implemented at great expense, then used as little more than automated filing cabinets for personnel records. The promised high-quality reports fail to materialise, and queries seem to take as long to answer as in the days of manual record-keeping. Outside the HR department, very few people know of the existence of the system — or if they do, regard it as entirely HR-owned. Considerable literature exists on this subject, most of which draws attention to a lost opportunity, and attempts to analyse why HR has not made more of its chances (see Kinnie and Arthurs, 1996, for a useful summary).

Some HR practitioners react to this criticism by blaming the system (particularly the report generator) for failing to deliver. Line managers are also blamed for their failure to understand the reports they receive and their lack of knowledge about what the system contains. Others have a sneaking suspicion that the criticism is at least partly justified, and that they have failed to make the most of the opportunities offered by the system. This may be due to some extent to a lack of vision within HR. However, it could also be interpreted as a failure of the organisation to realise that the implementation of a corporate HR information system, designed to support strategic decision-making, is in fact a major organisational change which is too big to be left in the hands of the HR function alone (Kossek *et al.*, 1994).

Why is implementation always so painful?

Unfortunately, the history of HR information system implementations is littered with examples of failure, time-table overrun and technical hitches. When the system at last goes live, the reality often fails to live up the hype. Several factors seems to contribute towards a general feeling of frustration and disillusionment.

- Expectations are raised too high, and too early. All sorts of promises are made — particularly about the quality of information, and ease of access by line managers — which do not materialise, or arrive much too late.

- Organisational factors — politics, culture and stakeholders — are not taken into account, or are given insufficient attention. In particular, a failure to identify champions and bring potential 'enemies' on board at an early stage leads to the project being managed at too low a level in the organisation, by individuals who have insufficient clout to overcome the inevitable difficulties that will arise. Inadequate resources for implementation compound the problem.

- A concentration on detailed processes, rather than best practice, often leads to a belief that the system must be customised to suit the organisation. Customisation always leads to massive delays and extra expense, as requirements are collected, analysed, misunderstood, re-analysed, programmed, tested, re-tested — and so it goes on. By this stage, the implementation process will have lost sight of the wood in its effort to perfect each individual tree. Not surprisingly, the rest of the organisation will soon lose interest. Even more depressingly, when the product is finally delivered with a fanfare of trumpets, the end-users (often not involved at all until the final stages of implementation), will probably not like it. Indeed, the OASIG study (1996) found that the failure to involve users in system development has major adverse effects on subsequent performance.

At last, a glimmer of light

To end on a more optimistic note, there is now evidence that the technology is beginning to deliver a different sort of HR information system, which may at last live up to the promises (see McNerney, 1996). Today's 'state-of-the-art' systems take advantage of client server technology and company intranets to involve all line managers — frequently, all employees — in the day-to-day running of the system. Line managers and individual employees are expected to manage their own personal data — but are also given the means to carry out this responsibility. The newer systems are also far more able to operate on an international basis (Sheppard, 1996). There seems to be hope that HR information systems will at last come into their own, freeing HR practitioners to take up a more strategic role and influence the business, while giving managers the tools that they need to generate the information to help them take decisions.

2 The Case Studies

Six large organisations were visited, and a variety of people in different positions, and at different levels, were interviewed and were allowed to offer any views they wished within a semi-structured framework. The discussions centred on six main areas.

- How was the system chosen, and who was involved in the decision-making process?
- The experience of implementation: was it good, bad or indifferent, and why?
- People and the system: in particular, any likes and dislikes, fears and suggestions for improvement.
- Use of the system day to day.
- The relationship between HR and IT.
- Is the system delivering to expectation? In what ways is it succeeding or failing?

Two of the organisations have given permission for their names to be used, while four prefer to remain anonymous for a variety of reasons.

CASE STUDY 1 : Halifax plc

This organisation is a leading company in the financial sector. It has a large headquarters, eight regional sites and around one thousand local sites. In addition to its core business, it has a Telebanking service (whose employees have their own terms and conditions) employing 450 people, a financial services arm with 1,500 employees and an expanding general insurance business. In all, the organisation employs around 30,000 people.

Case study visit

The following people were interviewed, either singly or in small groups, using a semi-structured discussion guide:

1. Group Personnel Manager, Personnel Systems
2. Payroll Manager
3. Manpower Planner
4. Personnel Systems and Support Officer
5. Remuneration and Benefits Manager
6. Employee Resourcing Officer
7. IT Project Manager
8. Implementation Manager.

Background

The current system

The organisation currently uses an in-house, self-built system, originally created in 1969 as a payroll system. Over time, various additions have been grafted onto the system to add personnel functionality. Although the system is reliable, and contains a considerable amount of detailed information about individual employees, it is perceived to have many disadvantages.

- It is labour-intensive, and therefore expensive, to maintain. At one stage, there were no fewer than 47 satellite systems with a link to the main system. These satellites add functionality to the main system, for example to allow users in the regional offices to access the system or a downloaded sub-set of data from the main system.

- It is inflexible, particularly with respect to reporting. Information users consistently complained about reports from the system, which have to be re-packaged into other formats in order to look presentable.

- It is not user-friendly, which means that users require specialist technical skills before they can access the system. Reports have to be ordered from a specialist team, and can take a week to be delivered.

- It does not lend itself to access by line managers, and is therefore perceived as a personnel records and payroll system rather than a management system.

- There are some problems with the accuracy of non-payroll data items, as data inputters often lack incentive to gather and maintain employee information — partly because they do not 'own' the information, and partly because some of it is rarely used.

Traditionally, IT resources tended to be directed towards 'front-end' systems, which have a customer interface; in organisational terms, Personnel has been a poor relation. The above dissatis-factions have existed for years, but did not surface as a priority until the arrival of a Personnel Director from another organi-sation. His perception of the inadequacy of the existing system kicked off the process to change, which ultimately led to a decision to purchase and implement a new system, PeopleSoft.

The new system

Justifying the decision to buy

The decision to start looking for a new system did not have to be justified formally to the organisation, due firstly to the obvious inadequacy of the current system and secondly to the personal presence of the new Personnel Director on the Board. However, a business case to justify the purchase of the new system was produced, and contained quantified benefits wher-ever possible. Two planned benefits are efficiency savings and increased data accuracy (which is expected to result from greater user-friendliness).

Evaluating the options

The organisation departed from its usual practice by deciding not to have a detailed specification of requirements, and not to self-build. Instead, an investigation of systems in the marketplace was carried out. A shortlisting procedure gradually whittled the choice down to two possibles, from an original list of 30. A de-tailed two-day workshop with both suppliers led to a unanimous decision to opt for PeopleSoft. The evaluation process to select the software supplier took six months, and was followed by a three month hardware evaluation, which led to the decision to purchase Hewlett Packard equipment.

Payroll

The PeopleSoft system does not yet have a payroll component. The anticipated release date for Payroll is 31 March 1998, and the organisation is to be a beta test site (which means that the software will tested by the organisation on its own site, using 'real' data, before release to other organisations). In the meantime, a link between PeopleSoft and the existing payroll system will be developed. The organisation decided to press ahead with implementation rather than wait for the payroll system to be developed, as the raised expectations generated by the prospect of having a state-of-the-art personnel system would otherwise be hard to manage.

Implementation resources

An implementation team (comprising 15 people) has been identified from a mix of Personnel, IT and Payroll staff, and is headed by an experienced project manager. Project resources include a suite of offices, a local area network and a training room.

Implementation plan

The main implementation steps are planned as follows:

- The first part of the system to be implemented was the **recruitment module**. The organisation needs to process around 50,000 application forms a year, and all recruitment administration is done centrally. The PeopleSoft system is being used in conjunction with a new optical mark reader, which has intelligent character recognition. The two main benefits of the new system are perceived to be the ability to monitor every stage of the recruitment process, and increased accuracy (due to greater user-friendliness).

- The core personnel system will be populated gradually, and departments will migrate across to the new system when they are ready. In the meantime, the 'old' system will be kept going.

- The interface between the existing payroll system and the PeopleSoft personnel system will be an urgent priority. Work in this area has to take place in conjunction with the task of populating the personnel system.

Implementation issues

The implementation team has already identified a number of issues that have the potential to hinder a smooth implementation.

- Managing expectations is likely to be a difficult task. After years of dealing (often at third hand) with an old and inflexible system, personnel practitioners are champing at the bit to explore and exploit what the new system offers. The implementation team has already identified around 700 potential users of the new system in Personnel alone. Before they can start to use the system, however, they need to:
  - be part of the new organisation-wide network, which is being implemented during 1997
  - be trained in both Windows 95 and the PeopleSoft system
  - assist in the population of the new system.

- Some people's jobs — particularly in Payroll and existing Personnel Systems support — will be threatened by the new system. This has not yet surfaced as a problem, particularly as the organisation has a policy of no compulsory redundancies. However, some employees may find themselves displaced, and may hold the new system responsible. Alternatively, some employees may take steps to find other jobs, which could result in the support team being under-resourced during the initial period when both the existing system and the new system are running in parallel.

- There is likely to be some tension between headquarters and the Regional offices and branches in the future, centred around who does what. Once the new network is in place, and all Personnel practitioners have direct access to the new system, it is likely that Regional and branch employees will start to question why so many Personnel activities should be carried out centrally.

- The implementation team is concerned that the roll-out plans for the system are sufficiently 'owned' by the organisation (despite high level support), and have a direct tie-in to the longer-term five-year plan for Personnel. There is a danger that a centrally devised implementation plan may not sit comfortably alongside the variety of Personnel projects that are currently under way.

Conclusions

The organisation is still very much in the honeymoon period as far as its new system is concerned, and it is very difficult to judge whether existing high expectations will be met. The support from the top of the organisation is encouraging, as is the willingness to commit implementation resources. Much depends on the smooth roll-out of the network, and the delivery of appropriate and timely training to system users. Personnel practitioners may need to play a more active part in owning the system, by participating in the implementation process rather than waiting for a working system to be delivered to them. It would also be very encouraging to see potential benefits identified and quantified in the five year plan.

CASE STUDY 2 : Government Department

The organisation is a government department with about 16,000 Group consists of about 2,000 staff, most of whom are based on a single site. The Pay and Pensions and the Accounts sections are located elsewhere.

The case study visit

The following people were interviewed, either singly or in pairs, using a semi-structured discussion guide:

1. Head of Development Policy
2. Project Manager, new HR information system
3. HR information systems Administration Manager
4. Head of Pensions and Payroll systems
5. Head of Personnel Administration
6. Two Personnel System users.

Background

Until the mid 1990s, the organisation used a mainframe personnel system that had been designed and built in-house for three government departments 15 years ago. The system was starting to show signs of age:

- It was unwieldy and inflexible.
- It was very labour-intensive and expensive to maintain.

- Non-standard reporting had to be done by a specialised team.
- It was designed to be used by three government departments, and ended up not entirely satisfying any of them.
- There were data quality problems with non-payroll-related data items.
- It was failing to deliver a variety of information now considered essential to the organisation, for example training records to support Investors in People.

Increasing dissatisfaction with the system coincided with the giving of notice, by the responsible government department, that the system would no longer be maintained after the financial year 1997/98. This spurred the organisation into action, and an evaluation process led to the selection of a new system, PeopleSoft, in November 1995. The new system was purchased for the Central Group, not for the whole Department. Three of the agencies also procured PeopleSoft solutions, two of them in a consortium with the Central Group. Other agencies have opted for separate solutions.

The new system

Evaluating the options

As a public sector government department, the organisation was bound by EU GATT procurement procedures. However, it took advantage of the new negotiated procedures route, which enabled it to go to the market with an outline of requirements, rather than a detailed specification. This saved time and enabled a much greater degree of flexibility — which proved invaluable, as requirements changed during the evaluation process. The organisation also took the decision to opt for minimum customisation, but to select a system which presented good personnel practice in the commercial environment.

An initial list of 15 possible suppliers was reduced to seven, and then three, before PeopleSoft was chosen. The organisation was helped through the procurement and evaluation process by a consultancy company.

The system runs on a UNIX operating system, using an HP9000 client server.

Three of the organisation's agencies have also opted for the PeopleSoft solution, but are implementing independently of the central group.

Justifying the decision to buy

Justifying the decision to purchase a new system was not difficult, as the old system was extremely expensive to maintain. A formal business case was made to the Director of Resources, containing three main justifications.

- The proposed new system scored higher than its competitors in the tendering process for a number of reasons. Cost was one factor considered in the process, as was ease of maintenance in comparison with the old system.
- There was considerable scope for better management information, due to improved functionality and much greater flexibility. Flexibility was a criterion identified very early in the planning stage as being essential.
- The technology used by the proposed new system was seen as enabling the delegation of routine personnel administration to the line, and therefore the reduction of the Central Personnel function.

Payroll

An interface was designed to pass information from the PeopleSoft system to the operational Pay Unit, which is geographically located elsewhere. Payroll records are prepared in the Pay Unit, then passed to the government payroll facility at Chessington for processing. This part of the project caused some difficulties, which have not yet been fully ironed out. The difficulties were mainly due to the fact that the interface was a customised product, rather than being part of the standard package. Initially, there were some misunderstandings, which meant that the Pay Unit did not always receive all the necessary information. The timescale was also very tight, so testing was very intensive. A massive effort ensured that the organisation went live to plan in July 1996, and has run payroll successfully since. The organisation is to be congratulated on this feat.

Implementation resources

The implementation project team (which consisted of the project manager, the systems administrator and representatives from the consultancy company, IT, Procurement and users) has evolved into a support and development unit to maintain the system and carry new developments forward. There is a full time systems administrator and a help desk facility for system users. Throughout the implementation there was a full time project manager. The Project Board (chaired by the Head of Personnel Administration) will continue, and will have a user group reporting to it. Throughout the evaluation and implementation process, PRINCE project management methodology was followed in principle, though not in detail.

Implementation plan

The system is now live as a central personnel records system, communicating with operational payroll. The Personnel, Absence, Recruitment and Appraisal modules are available for use now, and will be followed by Training Administration, Succession Planning and Manpower Planning. Currently, the number of users is very small, and is confined to Central Personnel. However, there are plans to roll the system out to the business units, so that business managers can use the system and start to maintain routine personnel records.

Implementation issues

Implementation is perceived by senior management in Personnel to have gone well. The feat of going live on time and within budget, within a very tight timescale, should be celebrated. The very accelerated implementation time-frame, combined with an unavoidable three month sickness absence of the key internal technical support resource, meant that some aspects of implementation (including user training) received less than ideal forward planning. The Personnel function was going through significant change at the time of implementation, with the delegation of a wide range of responsibilities to line managers and a re-structuring of the residual Personnel Unit. This meant that prospective users were not completely confident in contributing a 'user perspective' of their need for functionality, and of the workflow processes they wanted the system to support.

The organisation now faces more challenges to enable the system to be used to its full potential.

- Setting up the new system has helped to identify where there were errors in the data on the old system. The old system also did not contain all the data required by the organisation. It is therefore likely that a big data gathering exercise will be needed.

- There are some concerns in the organisation that jobs may be at risk as a result of the new system. This particularly applies in Payroll, where there are concerns that the operational Pay Unit may be bypassed in favour of a direct link between PeopleSoft and Chessington. However, Central Personnel jobs may also be threatened if routine personnel administration is passed to business units.

- The internal communications network (used for office auto-mation, particularly E-mail) has severely restricted the use of the PeopleSoft system. Initially, network failures tended to be confused with system failings, but users now understand the it is not the fault of the system when the network goes down. However, the PeopleSoft system has been designed to be used with a workflow system, without which it is unlikely to achieve its full potential.

- There are signs that users want to press ahead with the new system. It was described by users as potentially 'all singing, all dancing', but is currently being used very much as a basic personnel records system. Users want to be able to use the system to enhance the profile of Personnel and benefit the whole organisation.

Conclusions

It is early days as far as the organisation's use of the new system is concerned. The system is delivering against the specification for the initial stage of the project. To enable further development — particularly the maintenance of personnel records by business managers — some investment in the network will be needed. If, in the future, employees are to gain access to the system to maintain their own records, workflow and probably an intranet will become requirements. Any such developments would, of course, be subject to a business case before funds are made available. The delegation of responsibilities to business manage-ment also has considerable training and support implications for the system.

The organisation believes that the success it has had in launching the system reliably has been very much a product of the quality of the basic system — without home grown modifications — and its flexibility. These factors have enabled the organisation to continue to modify and develop the system in a way which might have been extremely difficult if it had procured a conventional product against a tightly defined user specification.

CASE STUDY 3 : Retail Organisation

The company is a household-name retail organisation, with stores all over the UK and in parts of Europe. There are about 50,000 permanent employees, plus up to 16,000 temporary and seasonal staff at any one time.

The case study visit

The following people were interviewed, either singly or in small groups, using a semi-structured discussion guide:

1. Project Co-ordinator
2. IT Manager
3. Personnel Executive (Personnel, Payroll and Pensions systems)
4. Personnel/Payroll Manager
5. Resource and Succession Planning Manager (Stores)
6. Assistant Manager, Recruitment
7. Personnel Manager, IT Group
8. System users: a Personnel Manager, two Personnel Assistants and a Personnel Secretary.

Background

The organisation uses Peterborough Software products for Personnel and Payroll. Until recently, Peterborough Software products were also used for Pensions and Recruitment. These systems were implemented in the late 1980s. At the time of purchase, the integrated Peterborough product was not available, so the organisation developed interfaces between the three Personnel, Payroll and Pensions products. Stores have their own bespoke system, which has an interface to the Peterborough Personnel and Payroll systems.

The current picture is changing, as the organisation has now moved to a new system for Recruitment (PWA) and is in the process of implementing a new Pensions system (Claybrook). A major review of Personnel practices and processes has begun, with a view to replacing the current Personnel system within the next three years.

Europe adds another dimension to the picture. Stores in France, the Netherlands and Germany have their own systems which, for different reasons, are in need of attention. The organisation is considering whether to opt for a greater degree of standardisation.

The current systems

Personnel and Payroll

The Peterborough systems are perceived to be payroll-driven and not very user-friendly. The organisation worked with Peterborough Software to develop 'UniVu' (a friendlier interface, allowing user access to relevant parts of the systems) and also an interface between the Stores and payroll systems.

The personnel system is reliable, and adequate for one-off queries. However, it is considered to have a number of disadvantages.

- It is not easy to produce reports, particularly aggregate reports, in the format required by managers.
- It is not user-friendly. 'UniVu', while easier to use, is difficult for users to access as they have to remember several different passwords. Users who persevere, however, are rewarded by higher-quality reports exported into Excel.
- Not all data items are date-related, so some changes to employee records have to be entered at the correct time in strict adherence to the payroll calendar.
- Historical information is perceived to be untrustworthy.
- It is inadequate for manpower planning purposes, which means that manual records have to be kept alongside the system to show details of management posts in the stores.

- Absence recording and reporting is considered inadequate, although very recently the organisation has introduced a spreadsheet for more detailed absence recording.

The payroll system has a rather better reputation. It is considered to be a stable and reliable system, although — due to heavy customisation — there can be problems when changes are made. Data accuracy is high, due to a comprehensive system of reconciliation and management control. The payroll system is likely to be the last to be replaced, probably around the year 2005.

Recruitment

Recruitment was seen to be a top priority for a new system because the old system was no longer performing satisfactorily. The organisation deals with around 18,000 application forms a year, nearly half of which are applications for the graduate scheme. The go-ahead for a new system was given in 1994, and the organisation selected PWA from a shortlist of four. The organisation took the decision not to customise unless absolutely essential, but to take the standard package system. The system 'went live' in the first week of September 1995.

The organisation is satisfied with the PWA system, which produces all the paperwork required by the recruitment process, and also does some screening of applications. Optical scanning is not currently used. The system may be extended into Europe.

The organisation is beginning to experiment with using the Internet for recruiting.

Pensions

A new pensions system became necessary when changes to the company pension scheme were agreed, and it became apparent that the existing system could not handle them.

The new Claybrook system, due to be fully implemented by July 1997, uses the latest technology — a workflow management system and document imaging. As with the recruitment system, the organisation decided not to customise, but to purchase a system that already mirrored good practice. There was a considerable amount of initial resistance to this approach, as people working in the pensions area had a preference for a system that would be written around existing practice. A project management approach that involved all users, however, achieved the necessary buy-in and resulted in considerable enthusiasm for the system. So far, implementation is on course.

The new personnel systems project

The organisation has launched a project to analyse rigorously current practices in personnel and training, as a precursor to replacing the existing Peterborough Personnel system around the year 2000. The current plan is to go out to tender for a new system early in 1998, and start working on the implementation of the chosen system by the end of 1998. The existing system is considered to be adequate in the meantime. A similar review of payroll practices is due to start in 1998.

The drivers for change

The push for a new personnel system has come from two directions. Firstly, system and information users have been pressing for change, as they perceive inadequacies and inflexibility in the existing system. Secondly, the Managing Director is a supporter of IT, provided it has a commercial justification. He has sponsored the Personnel Group's systems strategy, which started off the process of examining practices in all areas of Personnel.

The business justification

A business case is always required for the purchase of a new system. Every group in the organisation has a 'commercial road map' which defines the direction in which the group is moving. Every project — IT or otherwise — has to justify its place in the road map. Before financial approval is given, a business case must be made, which looks at the cost of:

- doing nothing
- upgrading
- replacing.

The 'do nothing' option is used as a benchmark. IT projects also have to meet the organisation's technical standards (client server and Windows). The organisation is moving away from customised and self-build systems, towards packaged solutions, and any 'wish lists' that cannot be accommodated within the standard package are challenged.

Conclusions

The organisation is taking a commendably measured approach to the selection and implementation of a new personnel system, and the review of existing practices should ensure that user requirements are rigorously defined. There are some issues that will need careful management.

- Personnel users of the existing system feel that they, and users of other systems at Headquarters, have had a poor deal in the past as far as IT resources are concerned. There is a perception, and perhaps a little resentment, that stores systems have taken priority.

- Some managers and departments are not, currently, able to use the e-mail or other facilities. Considerable investment will be needed if a state-of-the-art personnel system is selected, as these new systems usually require a workflow system and/or intranet to be used to their full potential.

- Personnel practitioners in the organisation are 'technology thirsty', particularly as they are now getting a taste (from seeing the new recruitment and pensions systems) of the possibilities. Managing expectations will be a huge challenge.

- The stores system currently interfaces with the personnel system. The organisation will need to look at the links between head office and the stores system — or possibly take a system that suits both needs.

- The organisation also faces the challenge of the European dimension — to standardise, or not? Several of the newer systems in the marketplace claim to be able to cope with global organisations, and the technology certainly exists.

CASE STUDY 4 : Subscription Services Limited

The organisation is one of the businesses belonging to a large public sector body. It has two main activities, the collection of television licences on behalf of the BBC, and a rapidly expanding telemarketing arm. There are about 1,600 employees, 950 of whom are based at Headquarters, with the rest in the field all over the UK.

The case study visit

The following people were interviewed, using a semi-structured discussion guide:

1. Personnel System Administrator
2. Employee Relations Officer
3. Personnel Administration Officer
4. Payroll Officer
5. IT Support Officer
6. Recruitment Assistant.

Background

The organisation uses the Peterborough PS2000 system for personnel and payroll. The payroll system has been in use since the end of 1992, and the personnel system since mid 1993. At the time of the evaluation (during 1991), PS2000 was judged to have the best available functionality, and was selected on that basis. The system has been heavily customised, due to the need to cope with public sector terms and conditions of employment.

The current system

Justifying the decision to buy

A business case was presented to the Board, which justified the purchase of the system on two main grounds, staff savings in Personnel, and improved quality of information. In the event, the expected staff savings have not occurred, because the system has not taken over routine processes as originally planned.

Implementation

The process to draw up a specification of requirements, evaluate systems in the marketplace, select a system and customise it was led by an outside consultant. Two full-time members of staff, one from Payroll and one from Personnel, were released from their jobs to support the consultant. Clerical assistance was also provided. Implementation resources were considered to have been adequate.

Support from the top of the organisation was very positive at first, but much less so when the project started to overrun; at this stage, the team was put under considerable pressure. The main reasons for the overrun were identified as:

- Unrealistic timescales at the start.
- Problems downloading data from the old system, as several data items were found to be corrupt.
- Data collection of new data items taking far longer than expected.
- Major difficulties with the customised parts of the system (such as occupational sick and maternity pay, temporary promotions, substitution and bulk salary updates).

There has been a very limited roll-out of the system to managers, in that all directors have read-only access, and some line managers in the telebusiness area are able to input staff sickness details.

System benefits

The system has now been in use for four years, and some benefits have been identified, particularly in the area of improved information.

- Information requests come from managers at all levels and parts of the organisation, and can usually be met from the system. The report generator (in the hands of someone who understands how to use it) is flexible.
- Information from the system has been used to inform decision-making and enhance the profile of the organisation. For example, information from the recruitment module has helped to inform recruitment drives, while the personnel system provided evidence to enable the organisation to gain the Investors in People award.
- The system is easy to use for quick enquiries about individual employees.

User perceptions

The **recruitment system** — which received very little customisation — is performing very well. The recruitment team handles about 10,000 applications a year, including internal transfers and promotions. Recruitment administration was previously a completely manual process; system users believe that the system has led to a much faster turnaround. The standard reports are easy to generate, and the transfer of the successful applicant to the main personnel system is also straightforward.

Users of the **payroll system** had rather mixed feelings towards it, and the overall feeling was one of disappointment that expectations had not been met. The good points were identified as:

- Straightforward to use, and faster than the old system.
- Ability to reverse and redo payroll, thus avoiding the need for supplementary runs.
- Ability to perform automatic month end reconciliation and auto balancing.

Set against these were the criticisms:

- User-defined reports are difficult to generate.
- User guides are not helpful.
- Parts of the system (the customised parts) do not work as they should.

The overall conclusion was that the system was slightly better than its predecessor, but not markedly so.

Personnel system users were very disillusioned with the system day-to-day, and some compared it unfavourably in some respects with the previous, in-house system. The main areas of criticism were:

- The report generator is hard to use and unfriendly.
- Parts of the system (the customised parts) still do not work as they should, and cannot be trusted.
- The system does not hold all the information required by Personnel — for example, accident statistics have to be recorded on a separate system.
- Some of the screens are not well designed.
- Network failures (though recognised not to be the fault of the system) cause intense frustration.

Personnel users were also very discontented with their share of IT resources generally; there was a perception that other parts of the organisation, such as Finance, had a better deal, and that Personnel was last in the queue.

Conclusions

The system has brought some benefits to the organisation, particularly in the area of better quality information. Users also believe that Payroll and Personnel staff have a much better understanding of each others' jobs as a result of having the system. Several problems, however, seem to be standing in the way of the system delivering to its original promise.

- The main difficulty lies with the customised parts of the system, which have never worked satisfactorily (it is interesting to note that the recruitment module, which was not customised, has been very well received).
- Another problem area is the report generator, which the average user finds unfriendly and difficult.
- The network is insufficiently robust to support the system.

Further investment in the network would help by reducing system down-time, but the difficulties with the customised parts of the system are unlikely to be resolved without a massive analytical and programming effort. A review of the whole system might be beneficial, as it would pinpoint more precisely what works and what does not, and enable decisions to be made about where remedial action should be targeted. User involvement with such a review is recommended, as users believe they were left out of the evaluation and selection process when PS2000 was originally chosen.

CASE STUDY 5 : National Utility

The organisation is a national utility supplier. There are 3,800 employees, most of whom are based at one of 14 regional sites. The headquarters has about 500 employees.

The case study visit

The HR Officer (Personnel systems and HR information) was interviewed, using a semi-structured discussion guide.

Background

When the HR Officer (Personnel systems and HR information) arrived two years ago, the organisation was using a variety of computerised personnel systems in its separate businesses, with little requirement for corporate personnel information due to the devolved nature of the organisation. In some instances, these systems have been gradually falling into disuse — particularly after the arrival of a new payroll system, which was implemented organisation-wide. An Executive Information System (EIS) has been created, using information from the payroll system downloaded on a monthly basis. There are around 35 users of the EIS, which is now the nearest thing the organisation has to a personnel system.

The current project

The organisation is in the process of selecting a new personnel and payroll system. The final selection has recently been made from a shortlist of four.

The driver for change

The current project was initiated by the new Director, who arrived with the organisation about a year ago, and was unhappy at the lack of a corporate personnel system.

Scope of the project

Initially, the project was confined to the selection and implementation of a stand-alone personnel system. The payroll manager had also identified that the payroll system would need replacing for a variety of reasons. The project has therefore acquired an additional dimension, and the organisation is looking for an integrated personnel and payroll system. The project team consists of representatives from HR, Finance, Internal Audit, Project Management and IT.

Approach to evaluation

HR managers and potential users were asked to draw up a list of requirements for the new personnel system, and the project manager (with assistance from a consultancy company) turned the 'wish lists' into a functional requirement. This emphasises the processes and reporting requirements to be carried out by the new system, rather than the data items to be held.

Around forty software suppliers were asked to provide information, and an advertisement was then placed in the *European Journal*. Supplier responses were judged according to the following criteria:

- functionality
- organisational technical requirements (client server, Oracle and UNIX)
- track record of supplier
- financial stability of supplier
- cost of system
- amount of risk involved (the lower the better).

From an initial shortlist of twelve suppliers, four systems were then identified for the final shortlist. The project team received demonstrations, went to user workshops run by the suppliers and visited user sites.

Justifying the purchase to the organisation

Following the normal rules on procurement, a scheme paper was drawn up, containing a cost benefit analysis and a business justification for the new system.

Implementation

Short term implementation plan

The payroll and personnel system is planned to be running live seven months after the selection is made. HR employees in the operating units will own the personnel data, and be responsible for maintaining personnel records. There will be no local customisation, although some flexible fields will be available for local use. Payroll will be run centrally, by an internal bureau.

Long term plan for the system

The organisation plans to have an intranet and to use workflow, enabling managers to take responsibility for some personnel data (for example, absence recording). Employees will be able to update their own personal details via the use of kiosks.

Implementation issues

Although the idea of having a new system is generally welcomed, some reservations are apparent.

- HR managers are somewhat cynical about the ability of personnel systems to deliver, given previous experiences.
- HR is not considered to be particularly IT literate, although there is considerable willingness to learn.
- Jobs may be at risk in both operational HR and Payroll. However, the organisation usually manages to achieve required staffing levels through its voluntary severance package.

Conclusions

The organisation is in the very early stages of implementation, and it is impossible to predict whether the vision for the future will be achieved. The decision not to customise is encouraging, as customisation nearly always seems to cause major difficulties and delays. Some attention to the network may be required if the system is to use a workflow system and an intranet to reach its full potential.

CASE STUDY 6 : Wandsworth Borough Council

The organisation is a Borough Council employing 5,500 people. Two thousand of these employees are school-based, and their personnel records are maintained elsewhere. The organisation's personnel system contains details of 3,500 current employees, with a variety of terms and conditions.

The case study visit

The following people were interviewed, either singly or in small groups, using a semi-structured discussion guide:

Principal Personnel Officer (responsible, among other things, for computerised personnel records)

Head of HR Services

IT consultant (in-house)

Personnel System Administrator

Five personnel system users.

Background

Since the early 1980s, the organisation has used a mainframe system originally developed by ICL (Personnel 29) and heavily customised in-house. It is not linked to the payroll system, although it produces paper outputs which are sent to the Payroll Department. Payroll services are currently provided in-house, after a period during which they were outsourced. ICL has announced that it will no longer maintain Personnel 29 after December 1998, so the organisation had to make a decision about the way forward.

The current system

Structure of the system

When the system was introduced in the early 1980s, it was Personnel's first foray into the world of IT; previous employee records had been maintained entirely manually. Probably as a result of this inexperience, the specification was extremely detailed, and required the system to hold a huge amount of data. There are eight modules:

- establishment
- employee
- absence
- recruitment
- training
- accidents and assaults

- job evaluation
- reference tables.

The establishment, job evaluation and reference tables modules are looked after centrally, while the employee, absence and accidents and assaults modules are maintained by Departmental Personnel. Maintenance of the recruitment module is shared; advertising is handled centrally, while Departmental Personnel deals with response and data input. The Training function, again with the help of Departmental Personnel, looks after the training module.

Implementation and post implementation

The implementation of the system is remembered as quite a demanding process, mainly because Personnel had very little understanding of the time it would take to collect and input data to the system. However, IT gave a lot of support, and the system went live approximately according to timetable.

When the Personnel 29 system was originally purchased, the organisation intended to give line managers access, but this has not come about — due partly to the system not being very user-friendly, and partly to the lack of interest displayed by line managers. As a result, it is seen predominantly as a Personnel-owned product.

Since the system was implemented, there has been a steady process of review, although this has not resulted in major changes. However, staff in both Central and Departmental Personnel remain committed to maintaining and using the system.

User perceptions

Users like some aspects of the system:

- the ease of accessing individual records
- the wealth of detail
- the amount of historical information that is held
- the attendance/absence monitoring facility is particularly comprehensive.

However, there are also frustrations.

- The existing report generator for non-standard reports is not user friendly, and it can take a long time to produce the required report.

- Changes to the system have to be approved by a number of people and scheduled into the IT work programme; this can take a long time.

- Although there is a good deal of satisfaction with some standard reports, others are not always appropriate for today's needs, but are difficult to get changed.

- There is no facility to record overtime or agency staff use, so additional systems have been devised for some departments.

The way forward

The organisation considered the option of switching from the existing system and purchasing a new one, but decided against this option. There were three main reasons. Firstly, the existing system meets most of the organisation's needs in terms of functionality, and its faults are seen to be mainly in the area of reporting. Secondly, the existing system has a considerable amount of historical data, which the organisation finds very useful, and which would be difficult to download to a new system. Thirdly, any new system would have to be customised due to the special nature of local government terms and conditions, and the organisation is aware of how problematical such customisation might be.

The organisation has therefore opted to keep its existing system, but migrate it to a new platform. It is to be converted to run on Windows NT servers in line with the organisation's IT policy, and will use Microsoft tools wherever possible (such as SQL). The conversion will be carried out by an external contractor, but the process will be managed in-house by IT and HR. The conversion will, it is hoped, overcome the previous problems with report generation, and should also give Departments more flexibility to maintain their own data. Departments will also be able to offer the system to line managers if they wish, so that some of the routine aspects of personnel record maintenance can be passed to the line.

Justifying the conversion

A business justification was put before the Council's Executive Board. The case was not difficult to prove, as the conversion option was cheaper than the purchase of a new system, and the risks of doing nothing (bearing in mind that Personnel 29 has a finite life) were obviously great. The Council, via the Executive Board, has endorsed the commitment to maintain a common area of data, and wholeheartedly approves the process of review.

Conclusions

The organisation's approach is an unusual one, but also one which has its attractions. If the conversion delivers as promised, the gains in terms of increased flexibility and much improved reporting will be considerable — and the existing functionality, and historical detail, will still be available. Employees in both Central and Departmental Personnel seem willing to work to make the conversion a success. The project is likely to be helped by the fact that there is a general acceptance that commercial systems are not suitable for the Authority without customisation, so cannot be purchased off the shelf.

Currently, there is not much interest in the system by line management, so it tends to be viewed as a Personnel-owned product. Running the system on a server may make it more accessible to line managers, but a change of culture may be needed before the line accepts responsibility for any personnel data. The local area network is apparently quite robust, but may require some attention if the system is to be made more widely available.

3 The Wider Picture

This chapter widens the discussion from the case studies to an examination of the results of a variety of recent surveys conducted on the theme of HR information systems. All the surveys referenced were reported in 1996 or 1997. They use different methodologies, and were commissioned for different purposes, but they nevertheless cast an interesting light on more general trends in the area of the use of IT in HR.

The IBM/CGI survey

This survey was based on interviews with 111 Payroll and/or Personnel Managers working in organisations employing more than 1,000 people. The sectors covered were spread over manufacturing, financial services, distribution, process manufacturing, government and utilities and oil and petroleum. Some key findings follow.

- The three most important factors when selecting HR information systems were:
  - functionality/flexibility
  - backup/systems support
  - product is tried and tested.
- Over three-quarters (77 per cent) of those interviewed stated that the pay-back period of the system was unknown. Fourteen per cent considered the pay-back period to be short, *ie* one to three years.
- The four most important benefits of having an HR information system were given as:

- easily able to produce statistics and process information (84 per cent)

- better reporting and more efficient enquiry handling (84 per cent)

- gives increased flexibility (82 per cent)

- improves the credibility of the HR/Payroll function (79 per cent).

● However, respondents also indicated that only 19 per cent of potential users outside HR use information provided by the system — and in only eight per cent of cases were systems providing management with information for decision making.

● It is also interesting to note that line managers are rarely involved in the selection of the system. This was stated to have occurred by only five per cent of respondents. Two-thirds of HR managers nevertheless believed *'better communications with line management'* to be a benefit of having an HR information system. It would be interesting to hear the opinions of the line managers!

● When asked about the information sources used to assist in the evaluation of HR information systems, the sources most frequently quoted by those with systems installed in the last two years were:

- trade press advertising/editorial (40 per cent)

- word of mouth (40 per cent)

- exhibitions/seminars (35 per cent).

● Only fifteen per cent had used user groups to assist in evaluation, and — worryingly — only ten per cent had used their IT Department.

The SOCITM IT trends 1996 survey

This survey, which focused on HR technology and usage in local authorities, was conducted by the Society of Information Technology Management (SOCITM) and reported in the January 1997 issue of *Conspectus*. The key findings are summarised below.

● HR information systems are widely used (in over 90 per cent of authorities). Nearly all systems hold basic employee and contract data, whereas qualifications, experience and training received were recorded in only about half.

● There was evidence of low IT investment in the past, in contrast to other departments (notably Finance). More encouragingly, nearly half of all authorities are currently planning to make major investments in new HR information systems.

- There was extensive duplication of HR data in manual and computer systems, with only sixteen per cent of authorities reporting no or little duplication.

- Line managers have on-line access to the HR information system in less than a third of authorities, and over 50 per cent of central HR departments rated the existing system as a poor or fairly poor tool for front-line managers.

- Respondents' comments indicated some mistrust of, and dissatisfaction with, IT practitioners and suppliers, and a belief that there was a lack of adequate software available.

- Some authorities wanted to take more advantage of newer technology (e-mail, the Internet, intranets), in various ways, for example:

  - advertising jobs on the Internet and accepting applications via E-mail

  - touchscreens within public access terminals or job centres to enter job applicant details

  - intranets to share policies and procedures.

The OASIG study

This study was carried out in the UK by OASIG, a Special Interest Group concerned with the Organisational Aspects of IT, and reported in 1996. It was based on in-depth interviews with 45 leading consultants, researchers and other specialists with expert knowledge of management and organisational issues. Their combined professional experience is said, by the authors, to cover approximately 14,000 organisations in all major sectors of the economy. The study explored all types of IT investments, rather than HR information systems alone, and as such could be considered not to belong to this report. However, the findings are likely to strike many chords with those familiar with HR information system implementations. Indeed, the findings may be quite encouraging to HR practitioners, in that they show that HR information systems are certainly not alone in presenting major challenges to organisations:

- 80 to 90 per cent of IT investments do not meet their performance goals.

- About 80 per cent of systems are delivered late and over budget.

- Around 40 per cent of developments fail or are abandoned.

- Under 40 per cent fully address training and skills requirements.

- Less than 25 per cent properly integrate business and technology objectives.

- Just ten to 20 per cent meet all their success criteria.

The OASIG study attempted to summarise the main reasons why IT systems fail. Some of their conclusions are presented below.

- Most investments in IT are technology-led. The major motive for investing in IT is to cut costs. These biases lead to a management agenda with too limited a focus on technological capabilities and efficiency goals.

- Most organisations therefore give inadequate attention to the human and organisational factors which are vital in determining the ultimate effectiveness of new systems.

- Users do not generally have a substantial or sustained influence on system development, which has major adverse effects on subsequent performance.

- Most senior managers do not have a good enough understanding of the links between technical and organisational change.

The 1997 Computers in Personnel survey

The annual Computers in Personnel survey is sponsored jointly by IES and the Institute for Personnel and Development. The 1997 survey drew responses from 194 organisations across a variety of sectors. Most respondents were from the HR function, and most were at manager or practitioner level within their organisation. Some of the key findings follow.

- The decision to purchase the system was usually taken either by HR (35 per cent of cases) or by a multi-disciplinary team (32 per cent). The IT department made the decision in only eight per cent of cases.

- HR is also the most likely function to be responsible for implementation (39 per cent), liaison with the system supplier (40 per cent), system training (57 per cent), security procedures (46 per

Figure 1: Responsibilities for CPIS activities

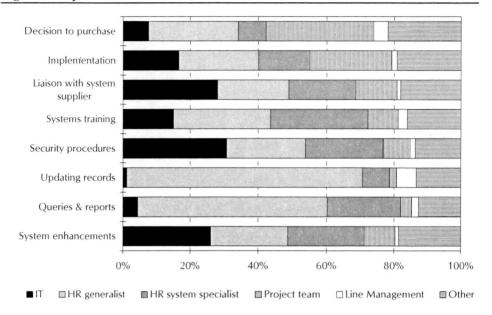

Source: CiP 97 Survey

cent), updating records (78 per cent), queries and reports (78 per cent) and system enhancements (45 per cent). Figure 1 illustrates these responsibilities.

- The activities most likely to involve IT are liaison with the system supplier, security procedures and system enhancements.

- The most important factors people look for when selecting an HR information system are:
  - user friendliness
  - ability to produce reports as required
  - flexibility
  - ability to integrate/compatibility with other systems
  - functionality.

- 74 per cent of respondents felt that, during implementation, they had commitment from senior management either always or most of the time.

- The most commonly identified future requirements are:
  - competency information
  - job or skill matching
  - Investors in People evaluation

The Institute for Employment Studies

- salary modelling
- 'what if' modelling.

- Less than half (46 per cent) of respondents stated that their organisation evaluated its use of IT in HR.

- When asked to respond to a range of statements about HR information systems on a five point scale, replies to the following statements suggested that there are some problems:

  - *'Personnel needs a better working knowledge of IT'* (76 per cent agreed or strongly agreed)

  - *'Upgrading poses problems'* (50 per cent agreed or strongly agreed)

  - *'The system is flexible to our changing needs'* (43 per cent disagreed or strongly disagreed)

  - *'Managers do not know what information is available'* (71 per cent agreed or strongly agreed)

  - *'The enquiry language is hard to use'* (48 per cent agreed or strongly agreed).

- On a more positive note, replies to the following statements indicate a greater degree of satisfaction:

  - *'Historical information is easily available'* (50 per cent agreed or strongly agreed)

  - *'Our users have the necessary IT skills'* (53 per cent agreed or strongly agreed)

  - *'Most of the data is accurate and up to date'* (74 per cent agreed or strongly agreed)

- Two-thirds of respondents indicated that their organisation would replace the current system in one to three years, or that this was currently being looked at. The most likely factors prompting this move (see figure 2) are:

  - to improve the quality of reporting
  - poor performance or inadequacy of the current system
  - devolution of HR responsibilities
  - integrating payroll
  - business re-engineering/cost efficiency.

Figure 2: Drivers for change

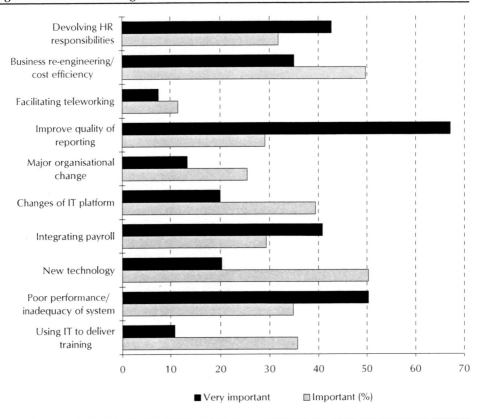

Source: CiP 97 Survey

The Institute for Employment Studies

4 The Supplier's Perspective

Representatives from four leading suppliers of computerised HR information systems were asked to give their comments on the implementation and use of HR information systems.

Implementation success factors

The suppliers are in broad agreement about what needs to happen to ensure a successful implementation.

1. **Give and take on both sides.** Suppliers must listen to clients — but clients must also recognise the experience of suppliers, which has been gained from dealing with many different organisations.

2. **Identification of the business benefits from the outset.** It is essential that the organisation identifies **measurable success criteria** (*eg* a reduction in absenteeism due to improved monitoring) and **monitors organisational performance against those criteria.** Unfortunately, this raises the issue of the lack of will of HR practitioners to monitor HR initiatives, or evaluate their worth to the organisation, for fear that they may not be able to justify their existence.

3. The need for **realistic timetables and adequate resources, in particular dedicated, full-time project staff.** The HR function has, according to suppliers, suffered from under-resourcing as far as IT is concerned — but there are signs that this is now changing.

4. HR practitioners must understand that packaged software now incorporates **best practice and best business process.** Organisations that insist on changing the software to match their processes, rather than examining their processes with a view to changing them, are treated with suspicion by suppliers.

5. A **procurement process that considers the needs of the whole organisation.** One supplier was particularly critical of constraining and unimaginative procurement processes, and stated that he would not touch the public sector for this reason!

6. A **buy-in from the whole organisation.** Today's HR information systems are far more than mere record-keepers, so the whole organisation must want and support the new system. Support from the top is particularly essential.

HR information systems day-to-day

Suppliers seem to accept that the newer HR information systems are very different from their predecessors — which they often term 'legacy systems'. Some suppliers believe that these 'legacy systems' are not delivering to their organisations, and are not capable of being much more than administrative record-keeping tools. Existing reporting tools are also acknowledged to be unfriendly and too technical. The newer systems require mechanisms to be in place to deliver organisation-wide access to the system — namely, e-mail, a company intranet and preferably workflow software. In order to get the best from the system, line managers need to be active users, while employees must become 'self reliant', via kiosks or direct intranet access. Line managers will not co-operate unless they see the benefits, which suppliers identify as rapid access to relevant information, and time savings in processing data directly, rather than via paper forms and manual flows.

Suppliers perceive that HR practitioners are now starting to buy in to the vision offered by newer systems, although there is some way to go. In particular, they need to loosen themselves from the constraints imposed by the older system model. Line managers, too, have a long way to go, as they have traditionally been reluctant to become involved with day-to-day HR activities — in contrast to the USA, where line involvement has become an established way of working. One supplier believed that such a change in established work patterns might need a very autocratic push in many organisations, before it could get off the ground. He knew of only two or three organisations who were, as he put it 'really getting their act together'. Another supplier was more optimistic, believing that there has been a big attitude change over the past year or so, particularly in the financial sector.

5 The Themes Revisited

This chapter returns to the themes identified in chapter two and asks whether they still stand, in the light of the evidence gathered from the case studies, the wider picture surveys and the suppliers.

Is HR under-resourced for IT?

Evidence from the case studies and the discussions with suppliers seems to support the argument that HR has traditionally not received its fair share of IT resources. In the public sector, the Finance function seems to have done best, while in the private sector any system with a customer interface has been given priority. Suppliers believe that this situation is now changing for the better, and the amount of investment currently occurring in the case study organisations supports their belief. The evidence from recent surveys (*eg* SOCITM and Computers in Personnel 1997) also indicates a high level of investment in IT, both now and in the next few years.

Are HR information systems IT-led?

In all the case study organisations, and in contradiction to the findings of the OASIG study, HR was firmly taking the lead in projects to select and implement a system. Evidence from recent surveys (*eg* IBM/CGI and Computers in Personnel 1997) also indicates that such projects are either led by HR or by a multi-disciplinary team. Indeed, the IBM/CBI survey seems to show a rather worrying trend away from any form of consultation with the IT function when evaluating HR information systems.

Suppliers consider that IT literacy in HR has improved considerably in recent years, and comments made during case study visits certainly support this view.

As far as payroll is concerned, the traditional high profile given to the payroll component of integrated systems seems to have evaporated. Instead, the HR part of the system is 'in charge', and provides the feeds to the payroll side.

Is there a business justification?

It is encouraging to note that all the case study organisations had produced a business justification — in fact, some were surprised that the question was even being asked. Most had followed a set pattern laid down by their organisations, which required them to identify and quantify costs and benefits. In this respect, HR is treated no differently from the rest of the organisation — although most admitted that some benefits (improved information quality was the most frequently quoted example) were hard to quantify. Suppliers, too, expect the organisation to produce a business justification, which identifies both the desired benefits and the monitoring criteria that will be used.

It is a little disappointing, however, that less than half the organisations replying to the Computers in Personnel 1997 survey evaluate the use of IT in HR.

Are job losses occurring?

Evidence from the case study organisations indicates that it is unlikely that the introduction of HR information systems will lead to job losses, even if the system also has a payroll component. Instead, jobs change, and usually become more rewarding, as individuals feel they are in a better position to cope with enquiries. Generally new systems are welcomed with a fair degree of enthusiasm — particularly by individuals who have been wrestling with inflexible mainframe systems for years. Payroll clerks, who are often at risk due to the current trend of outsourcing payroll, often see a new integrated system as a job saviour.

The continuing attempt to pass routine HR administration down the line has obvious implications for the loss of junior posts in HR, but HR information systems do not seem to be attracting any blame for this. It will be interesting to see if HR employees are quite so enthusiastic about their new systems if new technology really takes off, and use of company intranets and employee kiosks becomes the norm. One supplier believed that this new technology would have a very big impact indeed on HR jobs.

The line manager's role

There is little evidence from the case study organisations of managers becoming involved with HR information systems, aside from occasionally requesting information from them. These systems are still seen very much as the responsibility of HR to maintain. However, if the suppliers are to be believed, things are about to undergo a drastic change in organisations willing to accept and resource the new technology vision. How line managers react remains to be seen. They might be more than willing to use an intranet to access a truly friendly HR system — or they might take the view that HR administration is not their responsibility. Much will probably depend on the will of those at the very top of the organisation, as such a big process change is unlikely to happen without a major push, and can certainly not be brought about by HR alone.

Does involvement with systems damage a career in HR?

There is some evidence from the case studies that IT skills are not rated particularly highly in HR, and certainly do not comprise a core competency. Some individuals in the organisations visited had acquired a reputation for being HR information system 'techies', but the views of other HR people towards these individuals was somewhat ambivalent, and not always complimentary. It is interesting to note that a new sort of job, with an embryonic career structure, seems to be growing up in HR — often called something along the lines of 'Manager, HR systems'. Sometimes, such individuals will have people working for them at a more junior level, usually with an advisory and/or report-production role. The Computers in Personnel 1997 survey produced evidence that these jobs are quite common, and often sit in between HR and IT, with a reporting responsibility to both functions.

One encouraging fact emerging from the case studies is that the driver to purchase a new system often seems to be the arrival of a new HR Director, who considers a good system to be essential to the HR function, and is prepared to take Board level responsibility for the system. This development indicates that HR information skills may perhaps be entering a new phase in terms of their perceived value to the organisation.

Does HR have a vision?

The HR practitioners interviewed during the case study visits could certainly not be accused of lacking a vision. They had very positive and optimistic views of the future, incorporating employee kiosks, co-operative line managers and, as a result, a much higher profile for HR. However, there was not always a firm plan to bridge the gap between the reality of the present and the vision of the future. Most organisations do not have a company intranet, or kiosks, or even an e-mail facility for all their employees, and considerable investment will be needed before the necessary infrastructure to support the vision is in place.

A further difficulty is that the vision is not being shared with the rest of the organisation — and is not always being embraced wholeheartedly within HR itself. HR systems cannot fulfil their potential unless the whole organisation wants them to, which means a thorough review of existing procedures and a considerable degree of direction from the top.

Is implementation getting less painful?

Many of the difficulties usually associated with implementing a new system were present in the case study organisations, and can also be detected in the wider picture, as represented by the various survey results. However, there is also evidence that organisations are learning from past mistakes — their own and those of others — and that suppliers are giving more informed and higher quality advice.

- Reviews of existing HR processes are happening *before* the decision to purchase a new system is taken.
- Organisations are accepting best practice processes, as represented by sophisticated systems, wherever possible, and are not insisting on customisation unless absolutely necessary.

- The importance of good quality project management, and adequate project resources, are recognised.

- The need to have commitment and support from the top of the organisation throughout the project is also acknowledged.

- HR practitioners are becoming far more expert in managing expectations and communicating at the appropriate time.

On the down side, HR information systems are still seen as the property and responsibility of HR, rather than belonging to, and benefiting, the whole organisation. There is also evidence of inadequate involvement of system users, line managers and other non-HR stakeholders in the selection, evaluation and development stages.

So, is there hope for the future?

The answer would seem to be a definite yes. HR practitioners are more IT literate, more confident about leading HR information system projects and more knowledgeable about implementation success factors. Evidence for these assertions can be found from the case studies, the surveys and the views of leading suppliers. The technology is now starting to deliver, enabling a vision of the future which involves the whole organisation contributing towards, and using, an accurate, up-to-date, relevant and accessible HR information system. The challenge for HR is to help the organisation to transform this vision into a reality.

6 Some Practical Advice

This chapter distils the experience of the case study organisations, the evidence from the surveys and the opinions of suppliers into some practical lessons for organisations using HR information systems.

Review your processes

Firstly, define and review existing HR processes. Until this is done, any plan to achieve a vision for the future will be based on rather shaky foundations. The review can then form the basis for an outline user requirement for a new system, and as a means of comparing system processes with the those of your organisation.

Listen to your supplier

Your supplier may not understand the ins and outs of your company, but he/she will have considerable knowledge of different types of organisation and will also know what is considered good practice in different areas of HR. Do not insist on a customised product unless you really can prove that customisation would have a business benefit.

Justify your purchase

Even if your organisation does not require a business justification, do one anyway. It is good practice, and good discipline, and will help you to focus on the measurable benefits. It will also show that HR is as capable as any other function at justifying its actions.

Help your organisation to own the system

Firstly, do not even start the project unless everyone at the top of the organisation is fully committed to the system and considers it to be an organisation-wide tool, rather than something which is owned by HR. Secondly, if line managers are expected to input to the system, give them the means to do so — preferably, a company intranet (these are suitable for small organisations as well as giants). Thirdly, if your system is to be used by everybody, ensure that it is not selected and developed by HR project managers alone. End users, line managers and senior information users, for example, should all be included.

Manage your project

It is absolutely essential that the process to select, evaluate, develop and implement your system is managed properly and expertly, and that adequate resources are made available to the project manager. Remember, too, that 'going live' represents the start of the project as far as the organisation's use of the system is concerned — so guard against resources disappearing over-night. The system will need to be managed throughout its life with the organisation.

Guard against over-optimism

There seems to be general consensus that things always take longer, and cost more, than expected when implementing computerised HR systems. People are naturally optimistic, particularly at the early stages of a project when they are full of enthusiasm. The experience of the case study organisations indicates that a small amount of pessimism may be needed to prevent unrealistic project plans.

Value IT skills in HR

Although HR has come a long way in terms of IT literacy, there is still a tendency to undervalue these skills and to give 'softer' competencies more prominence. If the vision — involving managers in routine HR administration, thus freeing HR practitioners for higher and more rewarding activities — is to be achieved, however, the services of those 'techies' with an intimate knowledge of HR information systems will be essential.

Monitor and evaluate

HR practitioners are notoriously bad at monitoring, yet are increasingly being called upon to do so. The business justification is the obvious starting point, as it should contain identified quantifiable business benefits. Examples could be: reduction in sickness absence (due to increased and more effective monitoring); faster flow of joiners, leavers and amended contract information (due to greater system accessibility); more efficient processing of applications for jobs (enabled by new technology); reduction in the proportion of time HR employees are spending on routine administrative tasks; and an increase in data quality (due to greater user-friendliness). Use of the system (by whom, and how often) is another measurable indicator, which can help to show the extent to which ownership of the system is passing from HR to the whole organisation.

Glossary

beta testing   Testing software by a group of users.

client server   A computer (the server) containing shared resources (applications, programs *etc.*), which is accessed by other computers on a network (the clients).

e-mail   Short for electronic mail; a means of sending text to a specific person across a network.

end user   Or user for short; the person who actually uses the computer or system.

Internet   The world-wide computer network.

intranet   A network used within an organisation, which is linked to the Internet and is not limited by location or geography.

kiosk   Location at which employees can use a terminal or PC to access and amend their personal details on the HR system. Often interactive and always aims to be user friendly.

OCR scanner   Short for Optical Character Reader scanner; a device that can read written or printed text. Can be used to scan application forms or aptitude/psychometric tests.

operating system   Software that controls the general running of a computer (eg UNIX, DOS, VMS, 4GL, OS/2).

report generator   Software that produces reports from data sources without the need for programming.

workflow   Software to ease and enhance the flow of data across a network or Intranet.

References and Further Reading

References

Adams A (1996), *Maximising your people through technology* (survey), IBM/CGI

Clegg C, *et al.* (1996), *Failing to Deliver: The IT Performance Gap* (survey), OASIG

Kinnie J K, Arthurs A J (1996), 'Personnel specialists' advanced use of information technology. Evidence and explanations', *Personnel Review*, Vol. 25, No. 3

Kossek E E, Young W, Gash D C, Nichol V (1994), 'Waiting for Innovation in the Human Resources Department: Godot Implements a Human Resource Information System', *Human Resource Management*, Spring

Lambert R, Peppard J (1993), 'Information technology and new organisational forms: destination but no road map?' *Journal of Strategic Information Systems*, September

McNerney D J (1996), 'Workflow and self-service transform HR', *HR Focus*, March

Sheppard G (1996), 'International rescue', *Personnel Today*, 13 February

Wheatley M (1997), 'Road to new technology' (survey of local authority use of IT in HR), *Conspectus*, January

Further reading

Help for technophobes

Usbourne produces a series of guides intended for older children, but very informative and not condescending:

Guide to Computers

Computer Dictionary

The Internet for Beginners

Books for project managers

Brown M (1992), *Successful Project Management in a Week*, BIM/Hodder & Stoughton

Reiss G (1993), *Project Management Demystified: Today's tools and techniques*, E & FN Spon

IPD (1997), *The IPD guide to implementing a computerised personnel system*, IPD

General interest

Arkin A (1997), 'Network solutions', *People Management*, 23 January

Greengard S (1996), 'Finding time to be strategic', *Personnel Journal*, October

Hunter T L (1996), 'How client server is reshaping the HRIS', *Personnel Journal*, January

O'Reilly N (1997), 'Good connections', *Personnel Today*, 30 January

Sobkowiak R T, LeBleu R E (1996), 'Repositioning HR Information Systems — Empowering employees through information', *Information Systems Management*, Winter

Welch J (1996), 'A site-seeing trip into cyberspace', *People Management*, 30 May